Microsoft Outlook 2016
Keyboard Shortcuts

For Windows

By

U. C-Abel Books.

Table of Contents

Acknowledgement. v

Dedication vi

Introduction. vii

What to Know Before You Begin. viii

Short Forms Used in This Book and Their Full Meaning. .ix

Chapter 1

Gathering The Basic Knowledge Of Keyboard Shortcuts. ..1

Chapter 2

15 (Fifteen) Special Keyboard Shortcuts. 14

Chapter 3

Keyboard Shortcuts In Outlook 2016. 19

Keyboard Shortcuts For SmartArt Graphics. 19

Use The Keyboard To Work With The Ribbon..................24

Basic Navigation...27

Search 29

Common Commands...29

Mail 33

Calendar 35

People 37

Tasks 39

Print 40

Send/Receive 40

Views...41

Customer's Page..50

Other Books By This Publisher. 51

Acknowledgement.

U. C-Abel Books will not take all the credits for Microsoft Outlook 2016 keyboard shortcuts listed in this book, but shares it with Microsoft Corporation because some of the shortcut keys came from them and are "used with permission from Microsoft".

Dedication

This book is dedicated to computer users and lovers of keyboard shortcuts all over the world.

Introduction.

We enjoy using shortcut keys because they set us on a high plane that astonishes people around us when we work with them. As wonderful shortcuts users, the worst eyesore we witness in computing is to see somebody sluggishly struggling to execute a task through mouse usage when in actual sense shortcuts will help to save that person the time wasted. Most people have asked us to help them with a list of shortcut keys that can make them work as smartly as we do and that drove us into research to broaden our knowledge and truly help them as they demanded, that is the reason for the existence of this book. It is a great tool for lovers of shortcuts, and those who want to join the group.

Most times, the things we love don't come by easily. It is our love for keyboard shortcuts that made us to bear long sleepless nights like owls, just to make sure we get the best out of it, and it is the best we got that we are sharing with you in this book. You cannot be the same at computing after reading this book. The time you entrusted to our care is an expensive possession and we promise not to mess it up.

Thank you.

What to Know Before You Begin.

General Notes.

1. It is important to note that when using shortcuts to perform any command, you should make sure the target area is active, if not, you may get a wrong result. Example, if you want to highlight all texts, you must make sure the text field is active and if an object, make sure the object area is active. The active area is always known by the location where the cursor of your computer blinks.

2. Most of the keyboard shortcuts you will see in this book refer to the U.S. keyboard layout. Keys for other layouts might not correspond exactly to the keys on a U.S. keyboard.

3. The plus (+) signs that come in the middle of keyboard shortcuts simply mean the keys are meant to be combined or held down together not to be added as one of the shortcut keys. In a case where plus sign is needed; it will be duplicated (++).

4. For keyboard shortcuts in which you press one key immediately followed by another key, the keys are separated by a comma (,).

5. It is also important to note that the shortcut keys listed in this book are for Microsoft Outlook 2016.

Short Forms Used in This Book and Their Full Meaning.

The following are short forms of keyboard shortcuts used in this Microsoft Outlook 2016 Keyboard Shortcuts book and their full meaning.

1. Alt   -   Alternate Key
2. Caps Lock   -   Caps Lock Key
3. Ctrl   -   Control Key
4. Esc   -   Escape Key
5. F   -   Function Key
6. Num Lock   -   Number Lock Key
7. Shft   -   Shift Key
8. Tab   -   Tabulate Key
9. Win   -   Windows logo key
10. Prt sc   -   Print Screen

CHAPTER 1.

Gathering The Basic Knowledge Of Keyboard Shortcuts.

Without the existence of the keyboard, there wouldn't have been anything like keyboard shortcuts, so in this chapter we will learn a little about keyboard before moving to keyboard shortcuts.

1. Definition of Computer Keyboard.
This is an input device that is used to send data to the computer memory.

Sketch of a Keyboard

1.1 Types of Keyboard.

   i. Standard (Basic) Keyboard.
  ii. Enhanced (Extended) Keyboard.

i. **Standard Keyboard:** This is a keyboard designed during the 1800s for mechanical typewriters with just 10 function keys (F keys) placed at the left side of it.

ii. **Enhanced Keyboard:** This is the current 101 to 102-key keyboard that is included in almost all the personal computers (PCs) of nowadays, which has 12 function keys at the top side of it.

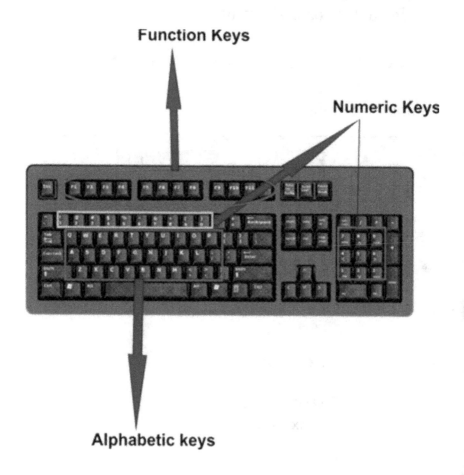

Function Keys

Numeric Keys

Alphabetic keys

1.2 Segments of the keyboard

- Numeric keys
- Alphabetic keys
- Punctuation keys
- Windows Logo key.
- Function keys
- Special keys

Numeric Keys: Numeric keys are keys with numbers from **0 - 9**.

Alphabetic Keys: These are keys that have alphabets on them, ranging from **A-Z**.

Punctuation Keys: These are keys of the keyboard used for punctuation. Examples include comma, full stop, colon, question marks, hyphen etc.

Windows Logo Key: A key on Microsoft Computer keyboard with its logo displayed on it. Search for this ⊞ on your keyboard.

Function Keys: These are keys that have **F** on them which are usually combined with other keys. They are F1 - F12, and are also in the class called Special Keys.

Special Keys: These are keys that perform special functions. They include: Tab, Ctrl, Caps lock, Insert, Prt sc, alt gr, Shift, Home, Num lock, Esc and many others. Special keys work according to the type of computer involved. In some keyboard layout, especially laptops, the keys that turn the speaker on/off, the one that increases/decreases volume, the key that turns the computer Wifi on/off are also special keys.

Other Special Keys Worthy of Note.

Enter Key: This is located at the right-hand corner of the keyboard. It is used to send messages to the computer to execute commands, in most cases it is used to mean "Ok" or "Go".

Escape Key (ESC): This is the first key on the upper left of the keyboard. It is used to cancel routines, close menus and select options such as **Save** according to circumstance.

Control Key (CTRL): It is located on the bottom row of the left and right hand side of the keyboard. They also work with the function keys to execute commands using Keyboard shortcuts (key combinations).

Alternate Key (ALT): It is located on the bottom row, very close to the CTRL key on both side of the keyboard. It enables many editing functions to be accomplished by using some keystroke combinations on the keyboard.

Shift Key: This adds to the functions of the function keys. In addition, it enables the use of alternative function of a particular button (key), especially, those with more than one function on a key. E.g. use of capital letters, symbols and numbers.

1.3. Selecting/Highlighting With the Keyboard.

This is a highlighting method or style where data is selected using the keyboard instead of a computer mouse.

To do this:

- Move your cursor to the text you want to highlight, make sure that area is active,
- Hold down the shift key with one finger
- Then use another finger to move the arrow key that points to the direction you want to highlight.

1.4 The Operating Modes Of The Keyboard.

Just like the mouse the keyboard has two operating modes. The two modes are Text Entering and Command Mode.

a. **Text Entering Mode:** this mode gives the operator/user the opportunity to type text.

b. **Command Mode:** this is used to command the operating system/software/application to execute commands in certain ways.

2. Ways To Improve In Your Typing Skill.

1. Put Your Eyes Off The Keyboard.

This is the aspect of keyboard usage that many don't find funny because they always ask. "How can I put my eyes off the keyboard when I am running away from the occurrence of errors on my file?" My aim is to be fast, is this not going to slow me down?

Of course, there will be errors and at the same time your speed will slow down but the motive behind the introduction of this method is to make you faster than you are. Looking at your keyboard while you type can make you get a sore neck, it is better you learn to touch type because the more you type with your eyes fixed on the screen instead of the keyboard, the faster you become.
An alternative to keeping your eyes off your keyboard is to use the *"Das Keyboard Ultimate"*.

2. Errors Challenge You
It is better to fail than not to try at all. Not trying at all is an attribute of the weak and lazybones. When you

make mistakes, try again because errors are opportunities for improvement.

3. Good Posture (Position Yourself Well).
Do not adopt an awkward position while typing. You should get everything on your desk organized or arranged before sitting to type. Your posture while typing contributes to your speed and productivity.

4. Practice
Here is the conclusion of everything said above. You have to practice your shortcuts constantly. The practice alone is a way of improvement. "Practice brings improvement". Practice always.

2.1 Software That Will Help You Improve In Your Typing Skill.

There are several Software programs for typing that both kids and adults can use for their typing skill. Here is a list of software that can help you improve in your typing: Mavis Beacon, Typing Instructor, Mucky Typing Adventure, Rapid Tying Tutor, Letter Chase Tying Tutor, Alice Touch Typing Tutor and many more. Personally, I recommend Mavis Beacon.

To learn typing with MAVIS BEACON, install Mavis Beacon software to your computer, start with keyboard lesson, then move to games. Games like ***Penguin Crossing, Creature Lab*** or ***Space Junk*** will help you become a professional in typing. Typing and keyboard shortcuts work hand-in-hand.

Sketch of a computer mouse

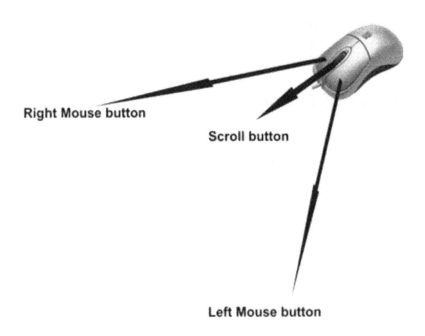

Right Mouse button

Scroll button

Left Mouse button

3. Mouse:

This is an oval-shaped portable input device with three buttons for scrolling, left clicking, and right clicking that enables work to be done effectively on a computer. The plural form of mouse is mice.

3.1 Types of Computer Mouse

- Mechanical Mouse
- Optical Mechanical Mouse (Optomechanical)
- Laser Mouse
- Optical Mouse

- BlueTrack Mouse

3.2 Forms of Clicking:

Left Clicking: This is the process of clicking the left side button of the mouse. It can be called *clicking* without the addition of *left*.

Right Clicking: It is the process of clicking the right side button of the mouse.

Double Clicking: It is the process of clicking the left side button two times (twice) and immediately.

Double clicking is used to select a word while thrice clicking is used to select a sentence or paragraph.

Scroll Button: It is the little key attached to the mouse that looks like a tiny wheel. It takes you up and down a page when moved.

3.3 Mouse Pad: This is a small soft mat that is placed under the mouse to make it have a free movement.

3.4 Laptop Mouse Touchpad

This unlike the mouse we explained above is not external, rather it is inbuilt (comes with a laptop computer). With the presence of a laptop mouse touchpad, an external mouse is not needed to use a laptop, except in a case where it is malfunctioning or the operator prefers to use external one for some reasons.

The laptop mouse touchpad is usually positioned at the end of the keyboard section of a laptop computer. It is rectangular in shape with two buttons positioned below it. The two buttons/keys are used for left and right clicking just like the external mouse. Some laptops come with four mouse keys. Two placed above the mouse for left and right clicking and two other keys placed below it for the same function.

4. Definition Of Keyboard Shortcuts.

Keyboard shortcuts are defined as a series of keys, sometimes with combination that execute tasks that typically involve the use of mouse or other input devices.

5. Why You Should Use Shortcuts.

1.   One may not be able to use a computer mouse easily because of disability or pain.

2.   One may not be able to see the mouse pointer as a result of vision impairment, in such case what will the person do? The answer is SHORTCUT.

3. Research has made it known that Extensive mouse usage is related to Repetitive Syndrome Injury (RSI) greatly than the use of keyboard.

4. Keyboard shortcuts speed up computer users, making learning them a worthwhile effort.

5. When performing a job that requires precision, it is wise that you use the keyboard instead of mouse, for instance, if you are dealing with Text Editing, it is better you handle it using keyboard shortcuts than spending more time with mouse alone.

6. Studies calculate that using keyboard shortcuts allows working 10 times faster than working with the mouse. The time you spend looking for the mouse and then getting the cursor to the position you want is lost! Reducing your work duration by 10 times brings you greater results.

5.1 Ways To Become A Lover Of Shortcuts.

1. Always have the urge to learn new shortcut keys associated with the programs you use.
2. Be happy whenever you learn a new shortcut.
3. Try as much as you can to apply the new shortcuts you learnt.
4. Always bear it in mind that learning new shortcuts is worth it.

5. Always remember that the use of keyboard shortcuts keeps people healthy while performing computing activities.

5.2 How To Learn New Shortcut Keys

1. Do a research for them: quick reference (a cheat sheet comprehensively compiled) can go a long way to help you improve.
2. Buy applications that show you keyboard shortcuts every time you execute an action with the mouse.
3. Disconnect your mouse if you must learn this fast.
4. Read user manuals and help topics (Whether offline or online).

5.3 Your Reward For Knowing Shortcut Keys.

1. You will get faster unimaginably.
2. Your level of efficiency will increase.
3. You will find it easy to use.
4. Opportunities are high that you will become an expert in what you do.
5. You won't have to go for **Office button**, click **New,** click **Blank and Recent** and click **Create** just to insert a fresh/blank page. **Ctrl +N** takes care of that in a second.

A Funny Note: Keyboard Shortcuts and Mousing are in a marital union with Keyboard Shortcuts being the head and it will be unfair for anybody to put asunder between them.

5.4 Why We Emphasize On The Use of Shortcuts.

You may never ditch your mouse completely unless you are ready to make your brain a box of keyboard shortcuts which will really be frustrating. Just imagine yourself learning all the shortcuts for the programs you use and its various versions. You shouldn't learn keyboard shortcuts that way.

Why we are emphasizing on the use of shortcuts is because mouse usage is becoming unusually common and unhealthy, too. So we just want to make sure both are combined so you can get fast, productive and healthy in your computing activities. All you need to know is just the most important ones associated with the programs you use.

CHAPTER 2.

15 (Fifteen) Special Keyboard Shortcuts.

The fifteen special keyboard shortcuts are fifteen (15) shortcut keys every computer user should know.

The following table contains the list of keyboard shortcuts every computer user should know.

1. **Ctrl + A:** Control plus A, highlights or selects everything you have in the environment where you are working.
    > *If you are like* **"Wow, the content of this document is large and there is no time to select all of it, besides, it's going to mount pressure on my computer?"** *Using the mouse for this is an outdated method of handling a task like selecting all, Ctrl+A will take care of that within seconds.*

2. **Ctrl + C:** Control plus C copies any highlighted or selected element within the work environment.

    > *Saves the time and stress which would have been used to right click and click again just to copy. Use ctrl+c.*

3. **Ctrl + N:** Control plus N opens a new window. *Instead of clicking* **File, New, blank/ template** *and another* **click,** *just press Ctrl + N and a fresh window will appear* instantly.

4. **Ctrl + O:** Control plus O opens a new program. *Use ctrl +O when you want to locate or open a file or program.*

5. **Ctrl + P:** Control plus P prints the active document. *Always use this to locate the printer dialog box and print.*

6. **Ctrl + S:** Control plus S saves a new document or file and changes made by the user. *Going for the mouse? Please stop! Don't use the mouse. Just press Ctrl+S and everything will be saved.*

7. **Ctrl +V:** Control plus V pastes copied elements into the active area of the program in use. *Using ctrl+V in a case like this Saves the time and stress of right clicking and clicking again just to paste.*

8. **Ctrl + W:** Control plus W is used to close the page you are working on when you want to leave the work environment.

> *"There is a way Peace does this without using the mouse. Oh my God, why didn't I learn it then?"* Don't worry, I have the answer, Peace presses Ctrl+W to close active windows.

9. **Ctrl + X:** Control plus X cuts elements (making the elements to disappear from their original place). The difference between cutting and deleting elements is that in Cutting, what was cut doesn't get lost permanently but prepares itself so that it can be pasted in another location selected by the user.

> *Use ctrl+x when you think* ***"this shouldn't be here and I can't stand the stress of retyping or redesigning it in the rightful place it belongs".***

10. **Ctrl + Y:** Control plus Y redoes an undone action.

> *Ctrl+Z brought back what you didn't need? Press Ctrl+ Y to remove it again.*

11. **Ctrl + Z:** Control plus Z undoes actions.

Can't find what you typed now or a picture you inserted, it suddenly disappeared or you mistakenly removed it? Press Ctrl+Z to bring it back.

12. **Alt + F4:** Alternative plus F4 closes active windows or items.

> *You don't need to move the mouse in order to close an active window, just press **Alt + F4** if you are done or don't want somebody who is coming to see what you are doing.*

13. **Ctrl + F6:** Control plus F6 Navigates between open windows, making it possible for a user to see what is happening in windows that are active.
   Are you working in Microsoft Word and want to find out if the other active window where your browser is loading a page is still progressing? Use Ctrl + F6.

14. **F1:** This displays the help window.

> *Is your computer malfunctioning? Use **F1** to find help when you don't know what next to do.*

15. **F12:** This enables user to make changes to an already saved document.

F12 is the shortcut to use when you want to change the format in which you saved your existing document, password it, change its name, change the file location or destination, or make other changes to it. It will save your time.

CHAPTER 3.

 ## Keyboard Shortcuts In Outlook 2016.

Definition of Program: Microsoft Outlook is a program designed by Microsoft Corporation that keeps people connected through its email services with powerful organizational tools.

The following list contains keyboard shortcuts that will boost your productivity in Microsoft Outlook.

Keyboard Shortcuts For SmartArt Graphics.

Insert a SmartArt graphic in an Office document

1. In the Microsoft Office program where you want to insert the graphic, press Alt, then N, and then M to open the **SmartArt Graphic** dialog box.
2. Press Up Arrow or Down Arrow to select the type of graphic that you want.
3. Press Tab to move to the Layout task pane.
4. Press the arrow keys to select the layout that you want.
5. Press Enter to insert the selected layout.

Work With Shapes In A SmartArt Graphic

TASK	SHORTCUT
Select the next element in a SmartArt graphic.	Tab
Select the previous element in a SmartArt graphic.	Shift+Tab
Select all shapes.	Ctrl +A
Remove focus from the selected shape.	Esc
Nudge the selected shape up.	Up Arrow
Nudge the selected shape down.	Down Arrow
Nudge the selected shape left.	Left Arrow
Nudge the selected shape right.	Right Arrow
Edit text in the selected shape.	Enter or F2, Esc to exit shape
Delete the selected shape.	Delete or Backspace
Cut the selected shape.	Ctrl+X or Shift+Delete
Copy the selected shape.	Ctrl+C
Paste the contents of the Clipboard.	Ctrl+V
Undo the last action.	Ctrl+Z

Move And Resize Shapes In A SmartArt Graphic

TASK	SHORTCUT
Enlarge the selected shape horizontally.	Shift+Right Arrow
Reduce the selected shape horizontally.	Shift+Left Arrow

Enlarge the selected shape vertically.	Shift+Up Arrow
Reduce the selected shape vertically.	Shift+Down Arrow
Rotate the selected shape to the right.	Alt+Right Arrow
Rotate the selected shape to the left.	Alt+Left Arrow

Notes:

- To apply more precise adjustments to shapes, press the Ctrl key in addition to any of the above keyboard shortcuts.
- These keyboard shortcuts apply to multiple selections as if you selected each item individually.

Work With Text In A SmartArt Graphic

TASK	SHORTCUT
Move one character to the left.	Left Arrow
Move one character to the right.	Right Arrow
Move up one line.	Up Arrow
Move down one line.	Down Arrow
Move one word to the left.	Ctrl+Left Arrow
Move one word to the right.	Ctrl+Right Arrow
Move one paragraph up.	Ctrl+Up Arrow
Move one paragraph down.	Ctrl+Down Arrow
Move to the end of a line.	End
Move to the beginning of a	Home

line.	
Move to the end of a text box.	Ctrl+End
Move to the beginning of a text box.	Ctrl+Home
Cut selected text.	Ctrl+X
Copy selected text.	Ctrl+C
Paste selected text.	Ctrl+V
Move the selected text up.	Alt+Shift+Up Arrow
Move the selected text down.	Alt+Shift+Down Arrow
Undo the last action.	Ctrl+Z
Delete one character to the left.	Backspace
Delete one word to the left.	Ctrl+Backspace
Delete one character to the right.	Delete
Delete one word to the right.	Ctrl+Delete
Promote the selected text.	Alt+Shift+Left Arrow
Demote the selected text.	Alt+Shift+Right Arrow
Check the spelling (not available in Word).	F7

Apply Character Formatting

TASK	SHORTCUT
Open the **Font** dialog box.	Ctrl+Shift+F or Ctrl+Shift+P
Increase the font size of the selected text.	Ctrl+Shift+>
Decrease the font size of the	Ctrl+Shift+<

selected text.	
Switch the case of selected text (lower case, Title Case, UPPER CASE).	Shift+F3
Apply bold formatting to the selected text.	Ctrl+B
Apply an underline to the selected text.	Ctrl+U
Apply italic formatting to the selected text.	Ctrl+I
Apply subscript formatting to the selected text.	Ctrl+Equal Sign
Apply superscript formatting to the selected text.	Ctrl+Shift+Plus Sign
Adjust the superscript/subscript offset up.	Ctrl+Alt+Shift+>
Adjust the superscript/subscript offset down.	Ctrl+Alt+Shift+<
Remove all character formatting from the selected text.	Shift+Ctrl+Spacebar

Copy Text Formatting

TASK	SHORTCUT
Copy formatting from the selected text.	Shift+Ctrl+C
Paste formatting to the selected text.	Shift+Ctrl+V

Apply Paragraph Formatting

TASK	SHORTCUT
Center a paragraph.	Ctrl+E
Justify a paragraph.	Ctrl+J
Left align a paragraph.	Ctrl+L
Right align a paragraph.	Ctrl+R
Demote a bullet point.	Tab or Alt+Shift+Right Arrow
Promote a bullet point.	Shift+Tab or Alt+Shift+Left Arrow

Use The Text Pane

TASK	SHORTCUT
Merge two lines of text.	Delete at the end of the first line of text
Display the shortcut menu.	Shift+F10
Switch between the **Text** pane and the drawing canvas.	Ctrl+Shift+F2
Close the **Text** pane.	Alt+F4
Switch the focus from the **Text** pane to the border of the SmartArt graphic.	Esc
Open the SmartArt graphics Help topic. (Your pointer should be in the Text pane.)	Ctrl +Shift+F1

□

Use The Keyboard To Work With The Ribbon.

Do tasks quickly without using the mouse by pressing a few keys—no matter where you are in an Office program. You can get to every command on the ribbon by using an access key—usually by pressing two to four keys.

1. Press and release the ALT key.

   You see the little boxes called KeyTips over each command available in the current view.

2. Press the letter shown in the KeyTip over the command you want to use.
3. Depending on which letter you pressed, you might see additional KeyTips. For example, if the **Home** tab is active and you pressed N, the **Insert** tab is displayed, along with the KeyTips for the groups in that tab.
4. Continue pressing letters until you press the letter of the specific command you want to use.

   Tip: To cancel the action you're taking and hide the KeyTips, press and release the ALT key.

Change the keyboard focus without using the mouse.

Another way to use the keyboard to work with the ribbon is to move the focus among the tabs and commands until you find the feature you want to use. The following shows some ways to move the keyboard focus without using the mouse.

TASK	SHORTCUT

Select the active tab and show the access keys.	ALT or F10. Press either of these keys again to move back to the Office file and cancel the access keys.
Move to another tab.	ALT or F10 to select the active tab, and then LEFT ARROW or RIGHT ARROW.
Move to another Group on the active tab.	ALT or F10 to select the active tab, and then CTRL+RIGHT ARROW or LEFT ARROW to move between groups.
Minimize (collapse) or restore the ribbon.	CTRL+F1
Display the shortcut menu for the selected item.	SHIFT+F10
Move the focus to select the active tab, your Office file, task pane, or status bar.	F6
Move the focus to each command in the ribbon, forward or backward.	ALT or F10, and then TAB or SHIFT+TAB
Move down, up, left, or right among the items in the ribbon.	DOWN ARROW, UP ARROW, LEFT ARROW, or RIGHT ARROW
Go to the selected command or control in the ribbon.	SPACE BAR or ENTER
Open the selected menu or	SPACE BAR or ENTER

gallery in the ribbon.	
Go to a command or option in the ribbon so you can change it.	ENTER
Finish changing the value of a command or option in the ribbon, and move focus back to the Office file.	ENTER
Get help on the selected command or control in the ribbon. (If no Help article is associated with the selected command, the Help table of contents for that program is shown instead.)	F1

Basic Navigation

TASK	SHORTCUT
Switch to Mail.	Ctrl+1
Switch to Calendar.	Ctrl+2
Switch to Contacts.	Ctrl+3
Switch to Tasks.	Ctrl+4
Switch to Notes.	Ctrl+5
Switch to Folder List in Folder Pane.	Ctrl+6
Switch to Shortcuts.	Ctrl+7
Switch to next message (with message open).	Ctrl+Period

Switch to previous message (with message open).	Ctrl+Comma
Move between the Folder Pane, the main Outlook window, the Reading Pane, and the To-Do Bar.	Ctrl+Shift+Tab or Shift+Tab
Move between the Outlook window, the smaller panes in the Folder Pane, the Reading Pane, and the sections in the To-Do Bar.	Tab
Move between the Outlook window, the smaller panes in the Folder Pane, the Reading Pane, and the sections in the To-Do Bar, and show the access keys in the Outlook ribbon.	F6
Move around message header lines in the Folder Pane or an open message.	Ctrl+Tab
Move around within the Folder Pane.	Arrow keys
Go to a different folder.	Ctrl+Y
Go to the Search box.	F3 or Ctrl+E
In the Reading Pane, go to the previous message.	Alt+Up Arrow or Ctrl+Comma or Alt+Page Up
In the Reading Pane, page down through text.	Spacebar
In the Reading Pane, page up through text.	Shift+Spacebar
Collapse or expand a group in	Left Arrow or

	Right Arrow, respectively
Go back to previous view in main Outlook window.	Alt+B or Alt+Left Arrow
Go forward to next view in main Outlook window.	Alt+Right Arrow
Select the InfoBar and, if available, show the menu of commands.	Ctrl+Shift+W

Search

TASK	SHORTCUT
Find a message or other item.	Ctrl+E
Clear the search results.	Esc
Expand the search to include **All Mail Items**, **All Calendar Items**, or **All Contact Items**, depending on the module you are in.	Ctrl+Alt+A
Use **Advanced Find**.	Ctrl+Shift+F
Create a Search Folder.	Ctrl+Shift+P
Search for text within an open item.	F4
Find and replace text, symbols, or some formatting commands. Works in the **Reading Pane** on an open item.	Ctrl+H
Expand search to include items from the current folder.	Ctrl+Alt+K
Expand search to include subfolders.	Ctrl+Alt+Z

Common Commands

Commands common to most views

TASK	SHORTCUT
Save (except in Tasks).	Ctrl+S or Shift+F12
Save and close (except in Mail).	Alt+S
Save as (only in Mail).	F12
Undo.	Ctrl+Z or Alt+Backspace
Delete an item.	Ctrl+D
Print.	Ctrl+P
Copy an item.	Ctrl+Shift+Y
Move an item.	Ctrl+Shift+V
Check names.	Ctrl+K
Check spelling.	F7
Flag for follow-up.	Ctrl+Shift+G
Forward.	Ctrl+F
Send or post or invite all.	Alt+S
Enable editing in a field (except in Mail or Icon view).	F2
Left align text.	Ctrl+L
Center text.	Ctrl+E
Right align text.	Ctrl+R

Format text

TASK	SHORTCUT
Display the **Format** menu.	Alt+O
Display the **Font** dialog box.	Ctrl+Shift+P
Switch case (with text selected).	Shift+F3
Format letters as	Ctrl+Shift+K

small capitals.	
Make letters bold.	Ctrl+B
Add bullets.	Ctrl+Shift+L
Make letters italic.	Ctrl+I
Increase indent.	Ctrl+T
Decrease indent.	Ctrl+Shift+T
Left align.	Ctrl+L
Center.	Ctrl+E
Underline.	Ctrl+U
Increase font size.	Ctrl+] or Ctrl+Shift+>
Decrease font size.	Ctrl+[or Ctrl+Shift+<
Cut.	Ctrl+X or Shift+Delete
Copy.	Ctrl+C or Ctrl+Insert **Note:** Ctrl+Insert is not available in the Reading Pane.
Paste.	Ctrl+V or Shift+Insert
Clear formatting.	Ctrl+Shift+Z or Ctrl+Spacebar
Delete the next word.	Ctrl+Shift+H
Stretch a paragraph to fit between the margins.	Ctrl+Shift+J
Apply styles.	Ctrl+Shift+S
Create a hanging indent.	Ctrl+T
Insert a hyperlink.	Ctrl+K
Left align a paragraph.	Ctrl+L
Right align a paragraph.	Ctrl+R

Reduce a hanging indent.	Ctrl+Shift+T
Remove paragraph formatting.	Ctrl+Q

Add links and edit URLs

TASK	SHORTCUT
Edit a URL in the body of an item.	Hold down Ctrl and click the mouse button.
Insert a hyperlink.	Ctrl+K

Create an item or file

TASK	SHORTCUT
Create an appointment.	Ctrl+Shift+A
Create a contact.	Ctrl+Shift+C
Create a contact group.	Ctrl+Shift+L
Create a fax.	Ctrl+Shift+X
Create a folder.	Ctrl+Shift+E
Create a meeting request.	Ctrl+Shift+Q
Create a message.	Ctrl+Shift+M
Create a note.	Ctrl+Shift+N
Create a Microsoft Office document.	Ctrl+Shift+H
Post to this folder.	Ctrl+Shift+S
Post a reply in this folder.	Ctrl+T
Create a Search Folder.	Ctrl+Shift+P
Create a task.	Ctrl+Shift+K
Create a task request.	Ctrl+Shift+U

Color Categories

TASK	SHORTCUT

Delete the selected category from the list in the Color Categories dialog box.	Alt+D

Flags

TASK	SHORTCUT
Open the **Flag for Follow Up** dialog box to assign a flag.	Ctrl+Shift+G

Mail

TASK	SHORTCUT
Switch to **Inbox**.	Ctrl+Shift+I
Switch to **Outbox**.	Ctrl+Shift+O
Choose the account from which to send a message.	Ctrl+Tab (with focus on the **To** box), and then Tab to the **Accounts** button
Check names.	Ctrl+K
Send.	Alt+S
Reply to a message.	Ctrl+R
Reply all to a message.	Ctrl+Shift+R
Reply with meeting request.	Ctrl+Alt+R
Forward a message.	Ctrl+F
Mark a message as not junk.	Ctrl+ Alt+J
Display blocked external content (in a message).	Ctrl+Shift+I
Post to a folder.	Ctrl+ Shift+S
Apply Normal style.	Ctrl+Shift+N

Check for new messages.	Ctrl+M or F9
Go to the previous message.	Up Arrow
Go to the next message.	Down Arrow
Create a message (when in Mail).	Ctrl+N
Create a message (from any Outlook view).	Ctrl+Shift+M
Open a received message.	Ctrl+O
Delete and Ignore a Conversation.	Ctrl+Shift+D
Open the Address Book.	Ctrl+Shift+B
Add a Quick Flag to an unopened message.	Insert
Display the **Flag for Follow Up** dialog box.	Ctrl+Shift+G
Mark as read.	Ctrl+Q
Mark as unread.	Ctrl+U
Open the Mail Tip in the selected message.	Ctrl+Shift+W
Find or replace.	F4
Find next.	Shift+F4
Send.	Ctrl+Enter
Print.	Ctrl+P
Forward.	Ctrl+F

Forward as attachment.	Ctrl+Alt+F
Show the properties for the selected item.	Alt+Enter
Create a multimedia message	Ctrl+Shift+U
Mark for Download.	Ctrl+Alt+M
Clear Mark for Download.	Ctrl+Alt+U
Display Send/Receive progress.	Ctrl+B (when a Send/Receive is in progress)

Calendar

TASK	SHORTCUT
Create an appointment (when in Calendar).	Ctrl+N
Create an appointment (in any Outlook view).	Ctrl+Shift+A
Create a meeting request.	Ctrl+Shift+Q
Forward an appointment or meeting.	Ctrl+F
Reply to a meeting request with a message.	Ctrl+R
Reply All to a meeting request with a message.	Ctrl+Shift+R
Show 1 day in the calendar.	Alt+1
Show 2 days in the calendar.	Alt+2
Show 3 days in the	Alt+3

calendar.	
Show 4 days in the calendar.	Alt+4
Show 5 days in the calendar.	Alt+5
Show 6 days in the calendar.	Alt+6
Show 7 days in the calendar.	Alt+7
Show 8 days in the calendar.	Alt+8
Show 9 days in the calendar.	Alt+9
Show 10 days in the calendar.	Alt+0
Go to a date.	Ctrl+G
Switch to Month view.	Alt+= or Ctrl+Alt+4
Go to the next day.	Ctrl+Right Arrow
Go to the next week.	Alt+Down Arrow
Go to the next month.	Alt+Page Down
Go to the previous day.	Ctrl+Left Arrow
Go to the previous week.	Alt+Up Arrow
Go to the previous month.	Alt+Page Up
Go to the start of the week.	Alt+Home
Go to the end of the week.	Alt+End
Switch to Full Week view.	Alt+Minus Sign or Ctrl+Alt+3
Switch to Work Week view.	Ctrl+Alt+2
Go to previous appointment.	Ctrl+Comma or Ctrl+Shift+Comma

Go to next appointment.	Ctrl+Period or Ctrl+Shift+Period
Set up recurrence for an open appointment or meeting.	Ctrl+G

See also under Views, Calendar Day/Week/Month view, and Date Navigator.

People

TASK	SHORTCUT
Dial a new call.	Ctrl+Shift+D
Find a contact or other item (Search).	F3 or Ctrl+E
Enter a name in the **Search Address Books** box.	F11
In Table or List view of contacts, go to first contact that starts with a specific letter.	Shift+letter
Select all contacts.	Ctrl+A
Create a message with selected contact as subject.	Ctrl+F
Create a contact (when in Contacts).	Ctrl+N
Create a contact (from any Outlook view).	Ctrl+Shift+C
Open a contact form for the selected contact.	Ctrl+O
Create a contact group.	Ctrl+Shift+L
Print.	Ctrl+P
Update a list of contact group members.	F5

Go to a different folder.	Ctrl+Y
Open the Address Book.	Ctrl+Shift+B
Use **Advanced Find**.	Ctrl+Shift+F
In an open contact, open the next contact listed.	Ctrl+Shift+Period
Find a contact.	F11
Close a contact.	ESC
Send a fax to the selected contact.	Ctrl+Shift+X
Open the **Check Address** dialog box.	Alt+D
In a contact form, under **Internet**, display the **Email 1** information.	Alt+Shift+1
In a contact form, under **Internet**, display the **Email 2** information.	Alt+Shift+2
In a contact form, under **Internet**, display the **Email 3** information.	Alt+Shift+3

Electronic Business Cards

TASK	SHORTCUT
Open the **Add** list.	Alt+A
Select text in **Label** box when the field with a label assigned is selected.	Alt+B
Open the **Add Card Picture** dialog box.	Alt+C
Place cursor at beginning of **Edit** box.	Alt+E
Select the **Fields** box.	Alt+F

Select the **Image Align** drop-down list.	Alt+G
Select color palette for background.	Alt+K, then Enter
Select **Layout** drop-down list.	Alt+L
Remove a selected field from the **Fields** box.	Alt+R

Tasks

TASK	SHORTCUT
Accept a task request.	Alt+C
Decline a task request.	Alt+D
Find a task or other item.	Ctrl+E
Open the **Go to Folder** dialog box.	Ctrl+Y
Create a task (when in Tasks).	Ctrl+N
Create a task (from any Outlook view).	Ctrl+Shift+K
Open selected item.	Ctrl+O
Print selected item.	Ctrl+P
Select all items.	Ctrl+A
Delete selected item.	Ctrl+D
Forward a task as an attachment.	Ctrl+F
Create a task request.	Ctrl+Shift+Alt+U
Switch between the **Folder Pane**, **Tasks** list, and **To-Do Bar**.	Tab or Shift+Tab
Undo last action.	Ctrl+Z
Flag an item or mark complete.	Insert

Groups

TASK	SHORTCUT
Expand a single selected group.	Right Arrow
Collapse a single selected group.	Left Arrow
Select the previous group.	Up Arrow
Select the next group.	Down Arrow
Select the first group.	Home
Select the last group.	End
Select the first item on screen in an expanded group or the first item off screen to the right.	Right Arrow

Print

TASK	SHORTCUT
Open **Print** tab in Backstage view.	Press Alt+F, and then press P
To print an item from an open window.	Alt+F, press P, and then press F and press 1
Open **Page Setup** from **Print Preview**.	Alt+S or Alt+U
To select a printer from **Print Preview**.	Alt+F, press P, and then press I
To **Define Print Styles**.	Alt+F, press P, and then press L
To open **Print Options**.	Alt+F, press P, and then press R

Send/Receive

TASK	SHORTCUT

Start a send/receive for all defined Send/Receive groups with **Include this group in Send/Receive (F9)** selected. This can include headers, full items, specified folders, items less than a specific size, or any combination that you define.	F9
Start a send/receive for the current folder, retrieving full items (header, item, and any attachments).	Shift+F9
Start a send/receive.	Ctrl+M
Define Send/Receive groups.	Ctrl+Alt+S

Macros

TASK	SHORTCUT
Play macro.	Alt+F8

Views

Table view

TASK	SHORTCUT
Open an item.	Enter
Select all items.	Ctrl+A
Go to the item at the bottom of the screen.	Page Down
Go to the item at the top of the screen.	Page Up
Extend or reduce the selected items by one item.	Shift+Up Arrow or Shift+Down Arrow, respectively
Go to the next or	Ctrl+Up Arrow or

previous item without extending the selection.	Ctrl+Down Arrow, respectively
Select or cancel selection of the active item.	Ctrl+Spacebar

Business Cards view or Address Cards view

TASK	SHORTCUT
Select a specific card in the list.	One or more letters of the name that the card is filed under or the name of the field that you are sorting by
Select the previous card.	Up Arrow
Select the next card.	Down Arrow
Select the first card in the list.	Home
Select the last card in the list.	End
Select the first card on the current page.	Page Up
Select the first card on the next page.	Page Down
Select the closest card in the next column.	Right Arrow
Select the closest card in the previous column.	Left Arrow
Select or cancel selection of the active card.	Ctrl+Spacebar
Extend the selection	Shift+Up Arrow

to the previous card and cancel selection of cards after the starting point.	
Extend the selection to the next card and cancel selection of cards before the starting point.	Shift+Down Arrow
Extend the selection to the previous card, regardless of the starting point.	Ctrl+Shift+Up Arrow
Extend the selection to the next card, regardless of the starting point.	Ctrl+Shift+Down Arrow
Extend the selection to the first card in the list.	Shift+Home
Extend the selection to the last card in the list.	Shift+End
Extend the selection to the first card on the previous page.	Shift+Page Up
Extend the selection to the last card on the last page.	Shift+Page Down

Move between fields in an open card

To use the following keys, make sure a field in a card is selected. To select a field when a card is selected, click the field.

TASK	SHORTCUT
Move to the next field and control.	Tab
Move to the previous field and control.	Shift+Tab
Close the active card.	Enter

Move between characters in a field.

To use the following keys, make sure a field in a card is selected. To select a field when a card is selected, click the field.

TASK	SHORTCUT
Add a line in a multiline field.	Enter
Move to the beginning of a line.	Home
Move to the end of a line.	End
Move to the beginning of a multiline field.	Page Up
Move to the end of a multiline field.	Page Down
Move to the previous line in a multiline field.	Up Arrow
Move to the next line in a multiline field.	Down Arrow
Move to the previous character in a field.	Left Arrow
Move to the next character in a field.	Right Arrow

Timeline view (Tasks)

When an item is selected

TASK	SHORTCUT
Select the previous item.	Left Arrow
Select the next item.	Right Arrow
Select several adjacent items.	Shift+Left Arrow or Shift+Right Arrow
Select several nonadjacent items.	Ctrl+Left Arrow+Spacebar or Ctrl+Right Arrow+Spacebar
Open the selected items.	Enter
Select the first item on the timeline (if items are not grouped) or the first item in the group.	Home
Select the last item on the timeline (if items are not grouped) or the last item in the group.	End
Display (without selecting) the first item on the timeline (if items are not grouped) or the first item in the group.	Ctrl+Home
Display (without selecting) the last item on the timeline (if items are not grouped) or the last item in the group.	Ctrl+End

When a group is selected

TASK	SHORTCUT
Expand the group.	Enter or Right Arrow
Collapse the group.	Enter or Left Arrow
Select the previous group.	Up Arrow
Select the next group.	Down Arrow
Select the first group on the timeline.	Home
Select the last group on the timeline.	End
Select the first item on screen in an expanded group or the first item off screen to the right.	Right Arrow

When a unit of time on the time scale for days is selected.

TASK	SHORTCUT
Move back in increments of time that are the same as those shown on the time scale.	Left Arrow
Move forward in increments of time that are the same as those shown on the time scale.	Right Arrow
Switch between active view, To-Do Bar, Search and back to active view.	Tab and Shift+Tab

Calendar Day/Week/Month view

TASK	SHORTCUT
View from 1 through 9 days.	Alt+key for

	number of days
View 10 days.	Alt+0 (zero)
Switch to weeks.	Alt+Minus Sign
Switch to months.	Alt+=
Move between **Calendar**, **TaskPad**, and the **Folder List**.	Ctrl+Tab or F6
Select the previous appointment.	Shift+Tab
Go to the previous day.	Left Arrow
Go to the next day.	Right Arrow
Go to the same day in the next week.	Alt+Down Arrow
Go to the same day in the previous week.	Alt+Up Arrow

Day view

TASK	SHORTCUT
Select the time that begins your work day.	HOME
Select the time that ends your work day.	END
Select the previous block of time.	Up Arrow
Select the next block of time.	Down Arrow
Select the block of time at the top of the screen.	Page Up
Select the block of time at the bottom of	Page Down

the screen.	
Extend or reduce the selected time.	Shift+Up Arrow or Shift+Down Arrow, respectively
Move an appointment up or down.	With the cursor in the appointment, Alt+Up Arrow or Alt+Down Arrow, respectively
Change an appointment's start or end time.	With the cursor in the appointment, Alt+Shift+Up Arrow or Alt+Shift+Down Arrow, respectively
Move selected item to the same day in the next week.	Alt+Down Arrow
Move selected item to the same day in the previous week.	Alt+Up Arrow

Week view

TASK	SHORTCUT
Go to the start of work hours for the selected day.	Home
Go to the end of work hours for the selected day.	End
Go up one page view in the selected day.	Page Up
Go down one page view in the	Page Down

selected day.	
Change the duration of the selected block of time.	Shift+Left Arrow, Shift+Right Arrow, Shift+Up Arrow, or Shift+Down Arrow; or Shift+Home or Shift+End

Month view

TASK	SHORTCUT
Go to the first day of the week.	Home
Go to the same day of the week in the previous page.	Page Up
Go to the same day of the week in the next page.	Page Down

Date Navigator

TASK	SHORTCUT
Go to the first day of the current week.	Alt+Home
Go to the last day of the current week.	Alt+End
Go to the same day in the previous week.	Alt+Up Arrow
Go to the same day in the next week.	Alt+Down Arrow

Customer's Page.

This page is for customers who enjoyed Microsoft Outlook 2016 Keyboard Shortcuts For Windows.

Dearly beloved customer, please leave a review behind if you enjoyed this book or found it helpful. It will be highly appreciated, thank you.

Other Books By This Publisher.

S/N	Title	Series
Series A: Limits Breaking Quotes.		
1	Discover Your Key Christian Quotes	Limits Breaking Quotes
Series B: Shortcut Matters.		
1	Windows 7 Shortcuts	Shortcut Matters
2	Windows 7 Shortcuts & Tips	Shortcut Matters
3	Windows 8.1 Shortcuts	Shortcut Matters
4	Windows 10 Shortcut Keys	Shortcut Matters
5	Microsoft Office 2007 Keyboard Shortcuts For Windows.	Shortcut Matters
6	Microsoft Office 2010 Shortcuts For Windows.	Shortcut Matters
7	Microsoft Office 2013 Shortcuts For Windows.	Shortcut Matters
Series C: Teach Yourself.		
1	Teach Yourself Computer Fundamentals	Teach Yourself
Series D: For Painless Publishing		
1	Self-Publish it with CreateSpace.	For Painless Publishing
2	Where is my money? Now solved for Kindle and CreateSpace	For Painless Publishing
3	Describe it on Amazon	For Painless Publishing
4	How To Market That Book.	For Painless Publishing